Luckily Fish Don't Need Raincoats

Written by:
Kevin Reese

Cadmus Publishing
www.cadmuspublishing.com

Copyright © 2021 Kevin Reese

Published by Cadmus Publishing
www.cadmuspublishing.com

ISBN: 978-1-63751-050-6

All rights reserved. Copyright under Berne Copyright Convention, Universal Copyright Convention, and Pan-American Copyright Convention. No part of this book may be reproduced, stored in a retrieval system, or transmitted in any form, or by any means, electronic, mechanical, photocopying, recording or otherwise, without prior permission of the author.

This is a work of fiction; therefore, names, characters, places, and incidents are the products of the author's imagination or are used fictitiously. Any resemblance to actual events, locales, or persons, living or dead, is entirely coincidental.

Dedicated to
My Grandmother
Bessie Harbor

Contents

Introduction 1
Kevin-Leroy 2
Swimming in caine 4
First of many Blessings 5
Loving Smiles 6
Educere 7
What Came Looking for me 8
The many mary's and paul's 9
A Riot on King Drive 10
Why did God teach us to swim? 11
A story told me by my uncle as told to him by the rain 12
Transferring pain 14
The universe will not be mocked 15
Deceits slumber 17
Certain days (an ode to the number 19) 18
Why did you stay so long? 20
I didn't do this alone 22
Wrap a taste 23
I''m a bit more revolutionary than you 24
Black fist and cold concrete 25
2wice the riser 26
HOW I 27
Velvet soul 28
That Poem 29
An ode to something I read about prison poems. (Dear Mr. Charlie) 30
2024 32
I'm From 33
I am a result of the things we water 35
Bronzille child 36
Village Makers 37
Everyone I loved 38
The Fourteenth Summer 40
I stood in the mossy grass and asked how did I get here? 42
18to32 44
Nov 2, 2020 46
Until We Are All Free 47

Introduction

"I need a motherfucker like a fish needs a raincoat!" - Bessie Harbor

This is what I heard from the first voice that I remember. The voice that taught me the most important lesson in life, and in my family this lesson was given as mandatory instruction for all of us to adhere to. We were taught that if "ONE GO WE ALL GO" my frame on collective liberation comes straight from my grandmother's garden of gems of light given to me so that I can take them with me everywhere I go. These poems are psalms of the light, I offer them to you as sacred.

So many folks to acknowledge, so I must start with saluting Minneapolis & Saint Paul the cities that I stand, breathe, and exist in every day.

Shout out to Voices For Racial Justice team/alumni/board and chosen family, it's an honor to manifest space, to advocate, and create a world that doesn't exist. I am a proud seed from this soil.

Shout out to the Minnesota Prison Writers Workshop (MPWW) salute to the entire team/alumni/board/instructors and all of our incarcerated chosen family. Special shout out to my homie and MPWW legend Ezekiel Caluiguri, who told me I was a writer before I ever started writing, I'm manifesting space in the city for Zeke's coming presence and energy "Sink or Swim and we been swimming our whole lives" - Zeke Caluguiri

Shout out to all of the artists, organizers, and humanitarians that I have had the privilege to hold space with, or be held in space with. I salute you all with the urgency of now.

I owe so much of my existence to art. These poems are my first small down payment.

KEVIN-LEROY

Crack was already in your system
If you were born on the southside in the 80's
You will always remember your uncle Jack
Smoking that devil trying to cure his cancer.
If you're lucky
You grow to be a man with sensibilities
And forgive him for stealing your
Sega genesis.
Even though you hated when
Grandma drank too much brandy
And cried for no reason.
You sure glad she taught you how to throw a jab
Spot a wooden nickel
And clean your long handled spoon
You hear enough Johnny Taylor
You learn that she cried because she knew, one day
You would have to remember everything she taught you.
Say, you don't catch a life sentence and completely lose your mind.
You come to appreciate your sister for trading in her childhood
For a wizard's wand that mystically produced you school clothes.
If it's in your cards you won't get shot in the face
And fall asleep on a train.
You get to hear your son say
Even though there is a cell bar between your hearts
He sure glad you ain't crazy and thanks
For his smile and charm.
You see these poems
Are psalms
Singing about Leroy
Cause I refuse to have some white man, or not right man, Write about me

LUCKILY FISH DON'T NEED RAINCOATS

Cause they will tell you all the things I was, Or all things I was not
But they will as sure as white is a lie
forget to tell you that all the while I was becoming.

Swimming in caine

Loretta
You were a genius
Using this cane
To help you stand
Help you retreat
Shovel snow in your eyes
To help you freeze the memories of summers past.

I, swam silently in place
Numb
You ran violently to this place
Numb, to me
Swimming silently in this place
Inhaling
the
Numb
I swam silently first
Rejecting, then accepting, then expecting

The numb.
Oh Loretta, you and them 80's Surely made me ready for the world

First of many Blessings

My suit was grey
The carpet was red
And our chairs circled the casket.

Everyone looked at me, whispered then cried.
Looked
Whispered
Then cried

But the carpet was red,
and its presence kept me in my seat.
So I sat.
And everyone
Looked at me then cried
Looked then cried.

And their tears were my only inheritance.

Loving Smiles

Before Hannah Montana
There was Pippi Longstockings
Living in our TV
Broadcasting from a world where all the kids had their own room.
We
Lived on 51st and woods
I
Had only a bowl a sippy cup with a hole
And a Pippi all my own.

Roaches and summer flies occupied our kitchen
But, my Pippi was brave.
With only my bowl
And her barrets for protection.

She would disappear
Then
Reappear
With my bowl, steaming rice, sugar cubes
And a stick of butter.

That's all we had, but it made us laugh, Because it's all we needed

Educere

To bring out, and bring forth.
Training my mind
Taming my creativity
With blue eyed history.
The death of my innocence
An emergent American
I entered this pipeline of fire
Vulnerable and raw
A sponge submerged in trauma
My first day, I pledged allegiance to the flag.
I finished every worksheet in record time
And received a blue eyed compliment.
This is where I learned I was black....
And one of the smart ones.

What Came Looking for Me

(2018 **AWP** award winner)

It was a whale-sized anchor,
eroded and stuffed inside a clamshell
forced down my throat
sinking in my saliva.
It was my uncle
chained to a Buick Skylark
eating a broken bottle
that shattered like my father's eyes
at the sight of his son sleeping in the womb,
barbwire attaching me to my mother.
It looked like my grandma's iron pot
boiling river water and collard greens,
and my calloused feet pacing a prison cell
with a wishing well adjacent to a metal bunk
with an elephant's tusk that sliced away follicles
of my skin every time I tossed and turned.
It was my son with an afro and a mustache,
standing in a field of snow with flip-flops
and no gloves, holding a basketball and a bus ticket.
It happened the day Minneapolis died
and a black rainbow galloped across the sky
and me and my cousins chased it.

The many mary's and paul's

My whole life I have glared across at mary
Waiting for her to tell me what paul said.
I would sit there, my grandma's kin, black and respectful.

Each time mary smiled and took in my respect as her inheritance
I grew poorer.
Each time
paul took my blackness as his inheritance I grew hateful

THIS HAS BEEN MY WHOLE LIFE.

I watched in agony
As paul and the night riders galloped away with my youth
mary said it was for my own good and my youth wasn't nothing but trouble.

(once every summer I get a unmarked postcard I suspect it's from my youth)

They would tie my hands
And throw corn at my feet
While screaming eat boy eat

I guess one day I will be free,
when
paul and mary grow a conscious
Or I get rid of mine.

A Riot on King Drive

Right here
In front of the liquor store
The world exploded
Fragments from a crack pipe
And a big wheel tire collided.
That created right now.
This destroyed grandpas hope
For manna during the famine.

The prayers failed us.

The horns have blown
The time has blitzed our strategies
And forced our plans into
The hands of today.

There is nothing left
But us and water.

Why did God teach us to swim?

I'm awake, still in this cell, folding myself into my own smile squeezing all my last tears into a puddle on the floor
To watch the moisture descended into the stone
It reminds me of the violence of water.
It's daunting, how water can make things weigh more, including moments.
It can splash and turn wishing for a big wheel into reading a PSI report.
The footing is slippery that's why I fill my shoes with plucked cotton from Q Tips
To preserve what I can. I also spit when I piss to maximize my offering.
I try to stay dry but a salt stuffed esophagus only craves one thing…
Survival is very practical in that way.
To survive you will learn to walk on elements that are softer than your feet.
You'll learn to scrape your fins on rocks until your scales spark into flames.

A Story Told Me By My Uncle As Told To Him By The Rain.

The original felony:

Kidnapping is a felony with a maximum prison
Sentence of 40 years. The survivors of such
horrific experiences are left with deep
Physical and emotional wounds these wounds
Take years to heal and too often, the victim
Never does.
I wonder will my fathers, fathers ever receive justice?
Will these wounds ever heal?

A story told me by uncle, as told to him by the rain.

I am not an immigrant
I've been kidnapped
My hands are froze
In cinder blocks of ice
I sleep
On a rusted blade
I count the suns
My tongue, is laden with wet cement
I feel like
Flesh
Being eaten by gnat teeth
I hear echoes
Of bones
Splitting on mountains
At the bottom of the sea, I see
Sharks swallowing marrow
Swallowing history
I suck salt water from wood

LUCKILY FISH DON'T NEED RAINCOATS

I'll die
To breathe
Breathe underwater
But breathe
And with my last breath
I will scream to the sky and join the rain

Kevin Reese

Transferring Pain

Telling lies with love
Tracing your steps to see where you lost it.
Kids on dirt roads picking up new bags
Filled with broken glass.
An american dictionary laced with the lovely language of lies.
Hospital rooms swelling with immense pressure
Will he make it?
Leaving who stayed, reading books that don't matter
Using the books that do to chop up cold cane
Crack pipes and brillo pads stuffed inside of cereal boxes
Empty cartons of milk remains of what was
Unexpected aggression like a storm on a parade
Serving a stray cat milk and wishing it leave you alone
Unanswered phone calls
Empty mailboxes
Having a bunch of left hand ideas in this right hand world
Adolescents drowning in pools, while toddlers stand by
The adults didn't teach them to swim.
The watchful eye of delayed gratification see's all
and reports the news.

The universe will not be mocked

The shards of glass that has become my wishes force my toes to mimic steel.
herd of unfortunates has been a barber chair to my beliefs
who can justify the mass herding of God's children into steel boxes
Or the mass production of steel cannons that is at the ready of every coward

who can eat veal with the profiteers who profit from the tears of hungry puppies
the surplus from years of exploitation will be the firewood that burns down happy land
everyone existing can feel, it's coming

So as a blessing I hold I'll send you with a bag of apples seeds and a screwdriver you do with it what you please

Who can call themselves a pimp and treat the earth like a working girl
what man cannot appreciate a working girl who works because of the lack of working man
do you want to make things better
how about you open every cell in the world, and let them sail the world

Pay Reparations!
Pay the workers more!
Pay the mothers more!
Pay the artist more!

How could you not love the people who invented jazz Question?
When was the last time you did something for the first time, and

the first time you did something for the last?

all noble men measure your worlds, include everything in it
so when you make decisions you include everything in it

The Summon Bonum vibrates my spirit dashing with the color
of Sunday mornings
defiant as happiness in the tomb
contagious as the rhythm of your favorite tune
taste as sweet as sugar cubes and grandma's coffee

Now Draw a line in the blood and let our yesterdays decide
your fate
Didn't I warn you
The universe will not be mocked

Deceits slumber

It's subtle
A light fragrance
Like wind blowing
Through vanilla beans
Descending on you like a warm hand on your skin.
Sometimes I wish I can hate
But im held in this skin
Forced to love, care, and cry
And take part in these savage festivities.

Certain days (an ode to the number 19)

Certain days have significance
Coincidence , and dreadful arrivals
The marks of paradigm shifts all around me.
On these days I remember
What it was like when I was
19
The place I was
And the places I wanted to be.

Certain days are like silk
Uninterrupted and divine
And some days
Are just the opposite..
On these days
I think of my father
And what parables
Got buried with him
That could have made it easier to be me.

Certain days sleep is gentle, and all my dreams seem true.
Then there are days
That snakes slither along my bed post
Searching for my eggs to eat.
On these days
I think of my son
And his precious black skin
And how I must protect his inheritance.

Certain days
I just wanna leave
To plant trees in liberia

And eat dinner off the oceans floor
And some days I wanna stay
To kick, punch, grab!
On these days I remember my name
Where I'm from and what I've been called to do.

Why did you stay so long?

700 days ago
You shifted
It's like a lone snowflake
Landed on our scale and
Tilted understanding out
Of our budget and made our love
Something we couldn't afford.

I watched in horror.

1,000 days ago you lied
I asked God to return my rib
And take back your creation
He laughed and told me to count my blessings

I never healed.

1,500 days ago we held Ke'vari
We talked when You conceived
you were fearful that I would leave
We decided to bless our blessing with the only thing
My father left me. (his last name)

I felt Immortal.

2,500 days ago when my grandma died, you unfolded my hand to swallow the tears from my palm. You prayed that God would manifest me into a better man so that when I came home the world would be a better place. I remember you sent a note that said max out on my canteen sheet and call you in the morning.

I felt like I was in my prime

3,500 days ago we said hello
I said you were kind, you told me I was Kevin
And you decided that you would reach through bars and share my pain as long as you could.

I felt selected.

Then on a cold morning in May it hit me.

Now I know.

Your belief in me kept me alive, and my faith in you helped you strive
And we gave each other a reason.

I DIDN'T DO THIS ALONE

(peace to everyone who kept me company, soothed my fears, and gave me confidence)

Today I woke up alone
Startled by chatter in the next room
Familiar voices
Discussing a catastrophe

I laid there paralyzed
The spine of my intentions crushed

I wish I would have let go
I actually have a platoon of wishes
That can't come to fruition, because
I'm alone
I'm startled
I'm paralyzed.

(thank you for reading this poem)

Wrap a taste

Let me drop an ant in your ear about the trap shawty
Its slow motion, you might have to start with a 8ball
The soil won't let you grow that okra you tilling
It's a distant lover to your ambitions
A sorry partna in this hand of spades
No truth at all

Let me breathe on you about the field ride
Wait until you see IT
It's a lioness losing her cubs to poachers for skin.
It's gon feel like the British is coming and your chief
Sell you from the village for a pouch of beans.
It's no fun G
Trust me
That's on 4nem grave

Let me build with about the bricks God
You know they want us all gone eventually
They closing down rikers island
Babylon is next
the boat just docked.

Let me balk with you about the turf blood
It's useless like the 40 that jammed when they shot up the function
Sad, like your first night on death row, and you hear niggas still repping the turf
And they will never see it again.

I"M A BIT MORE REVOLUTIONARY THAN YOU.

(some disrespectful shit said to me by an Old Head in 2017, but I love his existence. The last time I saw him he walked by me with handcuffs on, bloody knuckles, his head held up high swinging his dreads after beating up a correctional officer) -true story

Embracing that we will die.

Sowing our blood in our ancestral mannerisms
Forging empires with flicks of our tongue.

Chipping rocks into pyramids
Burning the crimson soaked hands who wish
To destroy us.
We transcend any circumstance
With songs that seep into our souls
And live in our strides forever.

"My way through movement is to practice the act of shining your light, We should measure our work by the people we have healed, be People who decide to be Free. The Movement is our Journey to Lead, and Embody Humanity. The Revolution will always be inspired by the People, and the Power with the People " - Kevin L

"Damn I Need To Check On Old Head He
He was actually a Great Writer"

Black fist and cold concrete

2pac said it!
He was the soundtrack
That spurred my determination
To conquer my adolescence

Rising through handcuffs, fighting against the darkness
Wrapped inside of a cocoon
With a lining as cold as last night.

Steel forges
With my imagination
Forges with my appetite
Until Steel becomes my contemplations.

My destiny is ancestral.
So when the moment come you can find me with my back
Against the concrete
And my black fists up to guard my chin.

2WICE THE RISER

Lucifer pierced some part of my soul
Chipped away some gold trinkets weakened my defense
I can't breathe is a sentiment for a tombstone.
I already lost too many days to chains.
Tomorrow is owned by no one
So I align my destiny to that.

HOW I.......

I was born dead,
2me's
One that white women wanted to hug, another that liberian women adored.
2me's
Cell#122 is not my name
It's what became of me
But my light is my own.
Born that way.
A forest green sapphire hatched out of my tribulations
I skated on some bloody blades
From fatherless to father
And created the language to explain it.

Velvet soul

To endure
Is like evading a ghost
And she is drawn to me because
I am a graveyard.

I am compromised
Holding my heart in my hands
Its all I have to barter
I'm empty of concessions..

I am afraid to view my remains
I am afraid.
I'm tortured by happiness
just tolerating myself
Bereaved by glee
I've seen it's mortality.

That Poem

I am a poet
And I'm jealous of poetry for its discipline.

Quick story:
It was a frightening experience.
God sent a bleeding coyote
To read me a poem
It said…

"You are a poet
Your world is a poem
And if you are ever lost
Look at the poetry around you
And you will find your way home"

An ode to something I read about prison poems. (Dear Mr. Charlie)

A poem don't mean nothing if it dont scrap its knees and bleed
Shake coves and make snow flash red.

What is a poem
If it dont laugh like a pack of hyenas
Crushing bones of gazelles

A poem ain't got no sauce, without one of the guys hustling under building
With some Jordan 6's on his feet and a razor blade under his tongue.

Fuck these poems
If they aint bloody boots on the couch
Or a handkerchief sewn out of bulls skin.

I can't personally stomach another poem that walks
English women across the street.
Listen Mr. Charlie don't toss me no damn poem written about no
Blue sky, red sox, or no white man.

A poem ain't worth a raindrop in a summer storm
If amalgamates it's steel or integrates its origins.

A poem should be the cracked kneecap of a runaway enslaved man
Barefoot and bleeding stumbling upon a pack of wolves.

A poem should freeze you black…
In the front of a barrel.

Any significant poem should be written with your left hand
With a subtitle like, (Fuck Norman Rockwell)
Chris Cabrera shit is better
With just spray paint and concrete he created the nile river.

And all of my poems I'm dedicating to Leroi Jones and Bobby Womack
And shipping them to chicago first.

KEVIN REESE

2024

This morning I ate a bowl of berries
Mixed in was sugar cubes
One dissolved on my tongue
The rush arrived like 2 missed phone calls both from her.
I sat in my kitchen on a metal stool
Staring into the corner
Watching a family of ants
Their silent movements reminded me of the time
We ate ice cream on my couch
While I scratched her legs.

Now I'm cleaning the ashes off the counter from the other day
When my homie dirty Tony
Stood in my kitchen rolling a blunt
With dirty nails and crisp white shoes
Asking me for a light, I pointed to the counter
He didn't see the lighter, but he did see my notepad
Of course he picked it up, "nigga you writing poetry?"
I wanted him to read it, but he lit the blunt instead.

Now it's just me and Bored of my company the ants began to take fragments
Of a pinto bean and fade into the wall
But two ants stayed eating ash
I wish I had their options.

I'm From

I am from the Crack smoke of the 80's and the gravel stuck under my mother's tongue.

I'm from the ghost of a child buried on 39th and King Drive next to the bronze resilience of Ida B Wells growing In my aunt's garden with the empty shell casings with no names.

I'm from the fingerprints in the jar of blue magic grease rubbed on my face coating in the sun.

I'm from stories originated under viaducts with Disciples Swinging chains in all white converses

I'm from the Dan Ryan expressway heading west, praying in the backseat of a car with no gas, facing the dawn of migration. I'm from the top of the sun forged into a lexicon of bones, dropped into a can.

I'm from the side of my grandma's bed opening a can of fruit cocktail whistling Andy Griffith.

I'm from the room next to my sister listening to SWV telling stories of returning from yonder.

I'm from the backyard, with a German shepherd and a stolen bike, next to the garage with a quarter pound in sandwich bags listening to the L.O.X.

I'm from the northside DEUCE SIX, right by the stop sign, 85 dimes in a cheetos bag, sold em
3 for 20 until I made my first knot.

I'm from my first cell in juvie slurping up vinegar at the bottom of my bowl of cereal.

I'm from the social workers office where I learned to not bring the business of white people into my family's home.

I'm from the court of plea bargains were we barter time for skin.
I'm from the cell next to where Jeff stands,
right above the phone, next to the pencil sharpener..

I'm from the soil, cultivated by the moon, stewards of the chosen, blinking in and out of consciousness.

I'm from the roll call for today, humming a melody called tomorrow.

I AM A RESULT OF THE THINGS WE WATER

I have come to the conclusion
that the WHITE man is the DEVIL
It is he alone.
Everybody else are givers
God has planted a beautiful life here
For me
and he is the only one
Trying to take it.

Kevin Reese

Bronzille Child

RowAfterRowAfterRow
Of homes, Families, Grandmothers
Who taught Bronze skin cousins
To never leave each other behind.

I learned my first lessons here
The Ida B Wells taught me, I oughta B, Bronze.
My skin is tattooed from BronzeSkinScrappingAgainstConcrete.

One morning, Nuck whooped my ass
My big sister looked on with copper pride.
That afternoon I found 1 dime
Bought 10 chews
Chewed 100 times.
That night I slept in the tub grandma told us to watch out for bullets coming through the walls

These bricks were the first thing to cut me
Opened my skin showed me my blood
And they branded me tribe.
So were our mothers, and so were their mothers.
Their prophecies birthed our bronze resilience.
And I'm resiliently moving with my
BronzeSkinisstillScrappingAgainstConcrete

Village Makers

(Featured in the 2019 Voices For Racial Justice Quilt Magazine)

Our neighborhood
is built on a slanted hill
and all traffic flow down.
Spirits
spike the air like crushed fiberglass
we all have strong forearms
from wringing out mops by hand.
Our grandmothers weave our clothes from collard greens, We
are matter, so collard greens are weaved from us.
It can always rain, so we are always weaving.
Our wrist ache at the mention of ships
and now, we are drums
weaved together with cedar wood and skin.
We transmit memory when we dance
remember...
We've built Capitol buildings before.
We bury our children teeth In the pasture
so their voices can grow.
Not change, but grow
we are not what we see
we are what we are

Everyone I loved

Me and my sister used to have picnics at Powderhorn park
Next to the pea green farm style water pump that sucked water from under the lake
And made every sip taste like turtle manure and dead goldfish.
Then.
The glaze from a honey bun wrapper was dessert and a half of beef and bean resers burrito was dinner. A clean towel to wash our face with would have made us feel like leaves in june
But all we had were ripped T-shirts.
Then.
I used to keep the insides of my forearms dirty, I think that's why my grandma put a dab of ajax and a blue cap of bleach in my bath water. I liked the dirt, so before my bath I would lick my thumb and rub back and forward across my forearm until the dirt rolled into small silos of clay that I would stick under my tongue.
Then.
I called Myself a caveman, I adopted the moniker from a family friend named BoScown
He and I shared the same birthday, he wore the same clothes for a year straight and whenever he would see me he would Holler Birthday Boy!! And give me all the change in his pocket.
Then.
I never thought about my father, until the summer of 98 when I was 12 and everyone I loved drove down to Chicago for a family reunion. I sat with my Big cousin B.C on the back porch of 70th and Morgan and drank a quart of cherry red Wild Irish Rose, Which tilted me sideways, Until I saw my Dad's obituary float down 71st street, and disappear on Emmet Till road.
Then.
I watched my grandmother while she slept. I built an altar for every breath, I could see my childhood in the drool that rolled down her cheek to rest on the mole on her neck. She was the

only thing between Me and my sisters growing up in foster homes behind squeaky doors with smeared fingerprints that would have made our smiles descend into our faces like bricks in oatmeal.
Then.
We all ate cabbage and salt pork out of the same pot and rolled up our pallets of wool blankets and put them in the same closet on top of black trash bags of winter clothes. We lodged nails in sticks that we kept by the wall, and we charged everything to the city like 100ft orange extension cords connected from the alley through the back door.
Then.
We were okra seeds, and smoked dripped from our eyes.
But now...

The Fourteenth Summer

June
I crashed into a metal door
not on purpose, but in the unintentional way one signs up for a robbery a week before Xmas and leaves with not the goods, but a bag of black bones.
It was my fault.
I know better than rushing through time that I purchased with skin.
It felt like the fuck you the door has been displaying for 13 years finally was spoken.
I embraced it
and stuffed my hands in my mouth to swallow the hurt. Skipped the chow hall, told my Queen not to visit the next day, you can't come into a prison visiting room with a black eye and say the door did it. but the door did do it,
the door did do it
I took a nap instead, I needed to be inspired, so I wrote
until the pages of my composition pad turned the color of freedom....... What color is freedom?

July
While in a phone line waiting to call rain
I drifted to a Vision of 20 fingers interwoven together
a covenant of companionship
anchored by a moment
sipping the champagne of loyalty
boasting of certainty
bursting with naivety
She didn't answer until the last day of the month.
It was the last time we would speak. I felt like a guitar with no strings.

August

LUCKILY FISH DON'T NEED RAINCOATS

I dreamed of owl wings and bowling balls for a week straight.
Every morning I awoke to a family of ducks praying outside my cell.
{They vibrated God}
I shaved my head while listening to my grandmother sing me a song

~Lord, Lord, Lord you know you been good to me~

I prostrated in silence
I seeked it.

For the first time I considered why I call myself black?
Why do we call ourselves death?
so I wrote myself Free.

Up ahead the glow from a punctured moon
and the silhouette of a woman motioned me forward.

I began to see the end.

I STOOD IN THE MOSSY GRASS AND ASKED HOW DID I GET HERE?

I held on to the taste of the butterscotch candy my grandma gave me at my dad's funeral.
I remember her hands.
She left me with warm wind
I was born a peace, a piece of them all.
When a liquor bottle shatter your fish tank as a child
You can become dangerous
liquor and broken glass is dangerous.

I been to school,
I learned a bunch of blue eyed stories.
I never liked how many people had control over my life.

Vanilla candles burned at my sister's house, I always felt safe there.
The smell of new shoes made me want to run,
I ran all the way to prison and back
And changed my shoes 1,000 times
I still change them mostly everyday.

I did push ups in cells and let me sweat seep into cement floors
I left my essence in so many rooms for free.
Despite… is such a spiteful word, it happens after your car is broken into
and you still make it home.

I smelled cigar smoke float over the hills during the famine. It was sweet. Smoke can be so sweet.
Now it's a question of breathing,
breathe in our indulgence and turn smoke into joy.

LUCKILY FISH DON'T NEED RAINCOATS

I started out pursuing justice, but justice is a frozen hammer of language.
Sentences are thawing bricks stuffed inside your pants,
Cold water still turns into mildew soaking in the soil of your shoes.
I touch my son every chance I get, it's his inheritance.
Our only inheritance is each other. I learned how to conjure warm wind
I melted gavels,
and walked in mildew soaked shoes until I made it here.

KEVIN REESE

18TO32

Damn, this world has fucked up my smile
Sped up my chill
Redirected me.
Freedom felt like sand through hands
That fucked me up
Left me in puddles, dirty as hell, cleaning the shoes of travelers.

I didnt know shit about having a woman,
or being in an adult relationship
and how tedious it was,
The requirement of paying attention,
it's difficult to be a good partner when you struggle with discipline
That sprouted.

My son has been a joy, but my scope on fatherhood
was being to my son,
what I wish my father could have been to me,
It worked for a while,
until I realized
What I wanted from my father was from the perspective of someone who didn't have his father to teach him discipline.
That sprouted too.

All my vices, the mindless shit I do.
Sprouted, Left me with too many people I'm responsible for.

The time I was 19, sitting in a cell,
wishing I could just go to school
a HBCU,
The parties I missed on campus,
The sister who would have taught me to open up doors
The chance to pledge a fraternity and learn some discipline

LUCKILY FISH DON'T NEED RAINCOATS

That sprouted too.

Born last, the runt of the pack
Leading the pride, blessed my heart,
That sprouted too.
The requirement of stewardship over my manifested self,
sprouted too
He kept me busy, ... skipping discipline.

Not being here to say goodbye
To my Grandma and all the legends
Who raised me,
sprouted too
It left me with pride
I visited them in the ocean

The cause and effect,
Of merely existing
Meaning you will be exposed to trauma
Sprouted too
Left me confused - healing on my couch.
Thinking... I did fly over the ocean.

Nov 2, 2020

Thinking about tomorrow,
looking at my schedule
Locking in visiting my niece and nephew
I wanna hold their arms and let them run their feet up my body
until they bounce off my chest into a flip landing on their feet.
I hope this grass is here for them to till
and my niece to grow flowers
I hope we build with bricks so my nephew can count them
I hope the air is here so they can breathe.

It's dark now,
and I'm thinking about death.
It's a dream and the backdrop is a tumbling society
I see boots, I feel guns
I feel hate.
I'm actually feeling violent today
tired of being abused, taking advantage of,
and the worst of them all ,
Vulnerable.
Existing as the same time as God
And at the same time as the Devil.

Until We Are All Free

Until we are all free,
We must all fight
We must unite
We must all light, whatever light we have.

Until We Are All Free,
We must stand against any system
That can only function if there is poverty and prison
Because in this system, with this thinking, none of us are free
So, as long as there is a cage for our children's dreams and a grave to muffle our children's screams, We. Are. Not. Free!

Now, I'm calling all the freedom fighters,
The Free-Dome Igniters
Unite with us.
The Brothers and Sisters, as we build this Bridge
Drowning at the bottom of the well
Using our Voices For Racial Justice
But, it's not just-us
And it's not just you
So Until We Are All Free
This is what we must all do.

We Must All fight,
We must all unite
We must all light, whatever light we have.

www.ingramcontent.com/pod-product-compliance
Lightning Source LLC
Chambersburg PA
CBHW071916070526
44583CB00016B/2021